Misnomers

D1254619

Misnomers

by Mark Dittrick and Diane Kender Dittrick
Illustrations by Henrik Drescher

COLLIER BOOKS • MACMILLAN PUBLISHING COMPANY • NEW YORK
COLLIER MACMILLAN PUBLISHERS • LONDON

Macmillan Publishing Company
866 Third Avenue, New York, N.Y. 10022
Collier Macmillan Canada, Inc.

Library of Congress Cataloging-in-Publication Data

Dittrick, Mark.
  Misnomers.
  Includes index.
  1. English language—Terms and phrases—Anecdotes, facetiae, satire, etc.   I. Dittrick, Diane Kender.   II. Drescher, Henrik.   III. Title.
PN6231.W64D5 1986   420.207   86-11794
ISBN 0-02-013670-6

Macmillan books are available at special discounts for bulk purchases for sales promotions, premiums, fund-raising, or educational use. For details, contact:

Special Sales Director
Macmillan Publishing Company
866 Third Avenue
New York, N.Y. 10022

Printed in the United States of America

Book design by Barbara Marks

misnomer   **1:** any dubious designation, inapt appellation, misleading label or other mistaken identifier that may already be in the dictionary (if you'll pardon the misnomer) but probably shouldn't be. **2:** a very appropriate name for this book, since every word defined in it—except, of course, for this one—is a misnomer.

Misnomers

black-and-white photography

a type of photography in which a roll of color film is loaded into a camera and then a picture is taken of something black and white, such as a nun riding a Zebra in a snowstorm, or a Franz Kline painting (as distinguished from taking pictures with noncolor—so-called black-and-white—film, which always results in a photograph composed of gradations of gray).

heavy cream a milk product containing between 30% and 36% milk fat, making a pint of it much lighter than a pint of light cream (about 18% fat); it's also much much lighter than an equal amount of skimmed milk (0% fat), the densest, and, therefore, the heaviest milk product of all, which is udderly amazing.

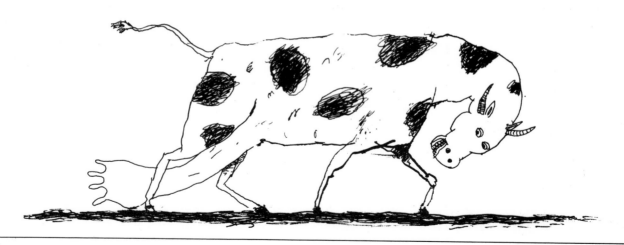

hit-and-run play   a play in baseball, wherein a runner at first base takes off like a lunatic for second base as the pitcher delivers the ball to home plate and *before* the batter attempts to hit the pitch in order to protect the runner.

chocolate chip cookie   an indigenous American cookie, formerly baked in home kitchens and tollhouses primarily, now a major component of the U.S. gross national product; invariably made with those little flat-bottomed drops (sometimes called morsels) of chocolate, *not* with pieces that have been chipped, chopped, lopped, or otherwise removed from a larger block of chocolate.

tortoiseshell

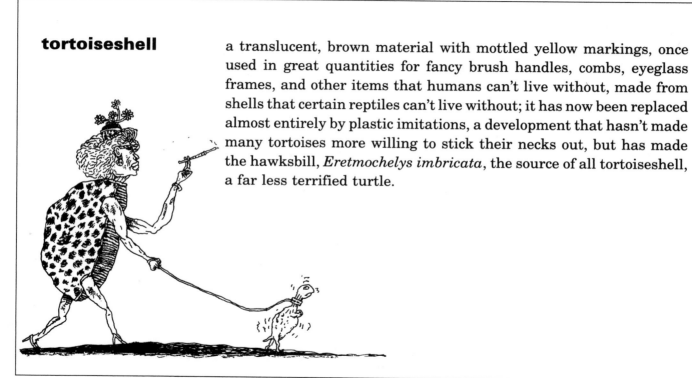

a translucent, brown material with mottled yellow markings, once used in great quantities for fancy brush handles, combs, eyeglass frames, and other items that humans can't live without, made from shells that certain reptiles can't live without; it has now been replaced almost entirely by plastic imitations, a development that hasn't made many tortoises more willing to stick their necks out, but has made the hawksbill, *Eretmochelys imbricata*, the source of all tortoiseshell, a far less terrified turtle.

Henry the Navigator

(1394–1460) a Portuguese prince who was so fascinated with the problem of how to sail out of sight of land without getting lost forever that he sponsored many early sailing expeditions, but not so interested that he ever got into a boat and gave it a try himself. Also called **Henry the Underwriter.**

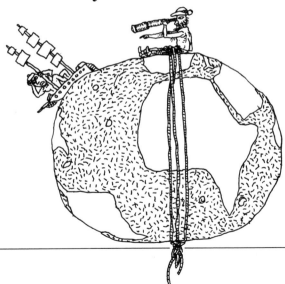

near miss a midair collision between two airplanes. *Seat-of-the-Pants Etymology:* assuming that the moment after two planes have avoided flying right into one another by a matter of millimeters, the pilot of one of the planes will probably turn to his or her copilot and exclaim, " ✦ ⚡ ! ⊚ ✗ , Roger, we nearly *missed* that ⊚ ! ✦ ⚡ ✗ ? ✦ ⚡ !" (*Note:* Since it is something of a euphemism, "near miss" may be only a near misnomer.)

walnut

the seed of a drupe, which botanically speaking is a fleshy fruit containing a hard pit that surrounds one to three seeds, and, therefore, is another noteworthy non-nut, produced by the English walnut tree, *Juglans regia*, which is not native to Great Britain and has never done particularly well there.

Brazil nut

another pseudonut that's only one of from 12 to 30 seeds that nestle like orange wedges inside a large coconutlike capsule produced by an evergreen tree, *Bertholletia excelsa*, that actually grows in Brazil.

coconut   a large, hard, hairy drupe seed that isn't likely to be found masquerading as a true nut, even in a Super Bowl–size can of mixed nuts.

peanut   the fruit (ripened ovary) of *Arachis hypogaea*, a leguminous plant related to peas and beans, that contains one to three edible seeds (*also* called peanuts), which can be turned into everything from salted peanuts to the dry-roasted kind; from sugar-coated airline nuts to peanut butter (chunky or smooth), and more—but *not* into true nuts (such as acorns or chestnuts), which are dry, single-seeded fruits that do not split open along a definite seam at maturity and that are enclosed in a woody or leathery shell.

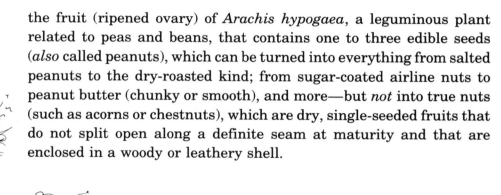

mixed nuts

a popular canned snack mixture typically containing around 98% peanuts, a few Brazil nuts, walnuts, almonds, pecans, and cashews, none of which are genuine, no-ifs-ands-or-buts nuts, and sometimes a couple of filberts (a.k.a. hazelnuts)—the only certifiable nuts in the bunch.

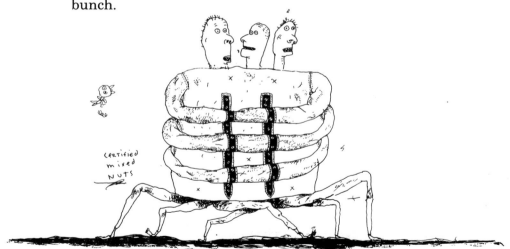

Certified mixed NUTS

spiral staircase   a winding staircase that would, if anyone could build one, transport a walker out and around in a two-dimensional path and eventually into a wall, and not from one floor to another, as does the three-dimensional helical staircase.

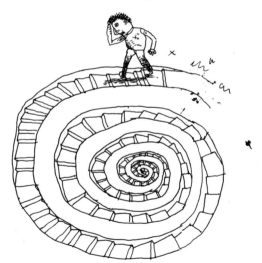

airline hijacking taken literally, the appropriating of an illicit or previously stolen airline, including all its planes, buildings, personnel, etc., and forcing the whole thing to make an unscheduled trip to somewhere like Havana (as distinguished from commandeering a single legitimate airplane).

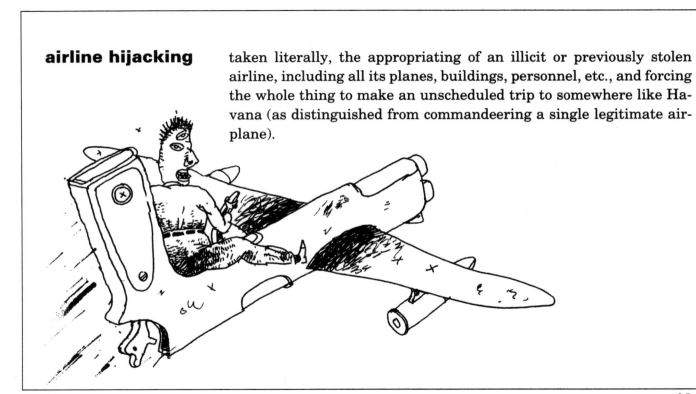

lightning bug   a small insect, *Photorus pyralis*, equipped with light-emitting organs on the underside of the abdomen; a shining example of a beetle erroneously called a bug.

firebug   an arsonist—a not-so-shining example of a person, *Homo sapiens pyromaniacus*, erroneously called a bug.

firefly   the erroneously named lightning bug erroneously called a fly.

fly-fishing   the sport of fishing with lures carefully tied by hand to resemble caddisflies, mayflies, stoneflies, damselflies, and other insects that aren't flies, in order to catch such fish as the brook trout, which is actually a char and not a trout.

hay fever   an allergic disorder caused by exposure to plant pollen and characterized by swelling and blockage of the nasal passages, headache, and frequent, violent, involuntary emissions of breath through the nose that are frequently followed by *Gesundheit. Misusage Note:* Although widely used, the term "is incorrect since hay is rarely implicated and fever is seldom present," says the *McGraw-Hill Encyclopedia of Science and Technology*, a reference that shouldn't be sneezed at.

chickenpox   a highly contagious disease, especially of children, that has nothing to do whatsoever with chickens; characterized by itchy rashes, fever, and headache, it is caused by the herpes zoster—that's "*zoster*," not "*roo*ster"—virus.

swollen gland   an abnormal enlargement of an otherwise normal enlargement of the body's lymph system, sometimes caused by a cold in the node.

side effect   a secondary effect produced by a drug, such as drowsiness resulting from taking a drug intended to dry up a runny nose; of course, if the very same drug is taken to cure insomnia, a severe case of super-duperdesiccated sinuses would be the side effect. (*Note:* In either case, operating heavy machinery should be avoided.)

fresh fish   fish found in a local fish store or in the fresh fish department of a supermarket, having gotten there as a result of being caught by some antiquated fishing boat, with no refrigeration equipment, that was probably out fishing for a week or more (as distinguished from *frozen fish*, which is usually caught by giant, modern factory ships that freeze their catches before they have a chance to stop flapping).

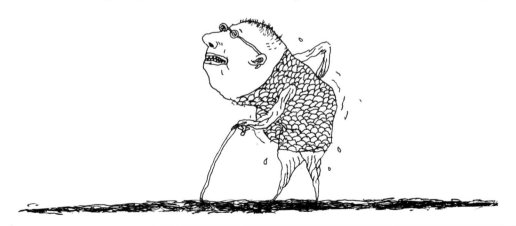

the human race

Homo sapiens, the human *species*, comprising many different peoples somewhat arbitrarily lumped together by anthropologists into relatively distinct groups that *are* properly called races.

the rat race

the sum total of all the activities engaged in by all the races of the human species.

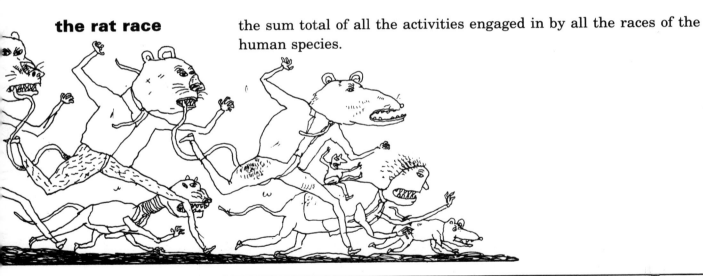

mankind   another inapt appellation for the human species, this time assuming it's populated entirely by men.

STRETCH WAIST

3 PIECE MATERNITY SUIT

COLLEAGUE WEARING A MACHO PAPOOSE

super glue   cyanoacrylate, an organic compound synthesized in the laboratory and used as an adhesive, noted for its amazing ability to instantly bond rubber, metal, plastic, the thumb and index finger, etc. *Misusage Note:* The term "glue," which correctly refers to any gelatinous adhesive made from the hide, hooves, bones, and connective tissues of animals, was carelessly applied to this material shortly after it was discovered in the late 1950s, and has stuck—like crazy—ever since.

dry cleaning   the cleaning of clothing in large revolving drums containing perchlorethylene or some other very wet solvent. (*Note:* Failure to employ this method to clean garments with DRY CLEAN ONLY labels sewn in them may result in a fine, imprisonment, or both.)

Coney Island   a neighborhood in New York City located at the southernmost point of Brooklyn and named for the many rabbits that once inhabited that part of the borough; known throughout the world for its amusement park, two-mile-long boardwalk, foot-long hot dogs, and for beaches teeming with bathers willing to bathe in waters teeming with bacteria; it's a phony island if ever there was one, which it wasn't until a tiny tidal creek was filled in a long time ago to attach what was never much of an excuse for an island to the mainland.

South Brooklyn   a neighborhood known throughout Brooklyn for being in the northern half of the borough, more than six miles north of Coney Island.

egg cream   a world-famous drink, invented somewhere in Brooklyn, that contains no eggs and no cream; made with milk, chocolate syrup, and a generous spritz of seltzer, it is not considered a genuine eggless, creamless egg cream unless the syrup used is Fox's u-bet®.

backbone   a bone in the back, especially any one of the 33 or so vertebrae that make up the spine; the fracture of any one of these is usually considered sufficient to break the entire back, whatever that is.

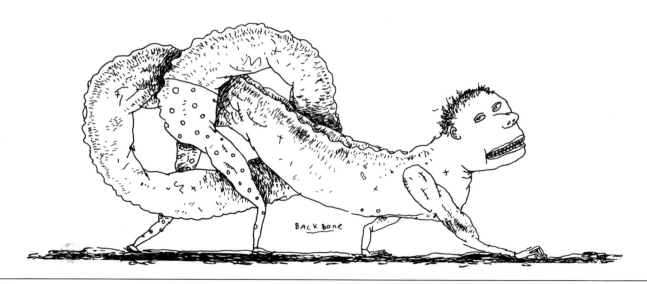

BACKBONE

moonlight   sunlight, at night, by way of the moon. In light of what sunlight's called in the daytime, sunlight at night ought to be called **nightlight.**

sunset   the diurnal descent of the sun below the horizon, if you're one of the few people who still believes the sun revolves around the earth.

sunrise   what the sun does every morning, if it still hasn't dawned on you that the earth revolves around the sun.

34

daylight saving time a system adopted by most states in the United States, whereby clocks are set an hour ahead in the spring in order to increase the amount of daylight in the day, a feat that has yet to be accomplished; this probably explains why people always set their clocks back to standard time in disappointment every fall, and why some states never adopted the system in the first place.

weightlessness
(as in *weightlessness in space*) the state or condition (or unrealistic diet goal) of having no weight at all, an impossible achievement according to Sir Isaac Newton, whose law of universal gravitation states that any body anywhere will still possess some weight unless it can get an infinite distance away from every other body in the universe, which simply can't be done, though, God knows, Garbo has tried.

perfect vacuum
1: a region that contains no matter, a theoretical place that doesn't exist no matter how far out in space you go; but, then again, nothing isn't perfect. 2: a machine used for cleaning the house that takes up no space in the closet, gets into every nook and cranny, has an endless cord that never gets tangled, and never, ever needs to be emptied.

empty space
any space between any of the pieces of matter that keep any imperfect vacuum from being perfect, and any space from being empty.

outer space
beyond the beyond?

Great Dane a large and powerful dog, considered by all the experts to be from Germany and not from some hamlet in Denmark. (To be or not to be, you see, does not seem to be in question.)

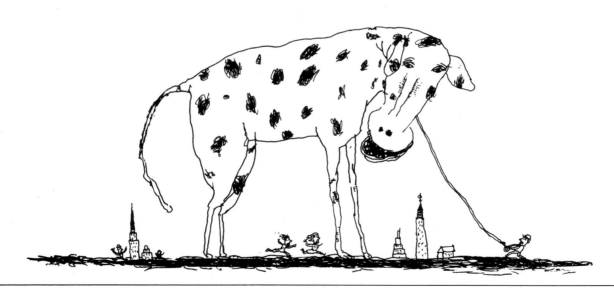

PAnama hAT hARVEST

Panama hat   a broad-brimmed hat, worn with white linen suits, made from the Panama-hat palm exclusively in Ecuador.

Panama-hat palm   a plant that is native to the American tropics, a perennial favorite for making Panama hats in Ecuador, and not one of the nearly 2,780 members of the palm family.

birthday party   a bash your proud parents threw to celebrate the first first day of the rest of your life, an event you've been celebrating with an anniversary-of-your-birthday party every year, ever since.

white wine   a type of wine that is nearly clear or pale amber or pale yellow in color, made from pale green grapes or from dark purple or dark blue grapes, from which the skins, pulp, and seeds have been removed. (*Milk* is white; so's a piña colada.)

radiator   **1:** a clanking, hissing, hollow, cast-iron device that warms a room by transmitting the heat from hot water or steam circulating within it to its outer surface by *conduction* and from there to the room on currents of air by *convection* and just a little bit also by radiating waves. **2:** a water-filled device, unknown to owners of Volkswagens, that cools an automobile engine mainly by *convection* as air flows across it.

Texas Panhandle   a region of northwestern Texas that doesn't even remotely resemble a handle, which hardly matters much since the rest of the state doesn't look anything like a pan; it's located just south of the western extension of Oklahoma, which looks exactly like a handle, and just west of the rest of Oklahoma, which looks a whole lot like a well-worn pan straight out of Julia Child's kitchen.

West Virginia   a mid-Atlantic state, none of whose residents lives farther west than the residents of Speers Ferry, Ben Hur, Keokee, Flat Gap, Bonny Blue, and quite a few other well-known towns in Virginia. Should probably be called **North Virginia**, or, at the very least, **North-Northwest Virginia.**

pronghorn antelope

a swift North American mammal, *A. americana*, that is the only living member of the family Antilopridae and not a true antelope, and not to be confused with *E. Americana*, which is an encyclopedia.

mountain goat

a not-so-swift but very sure-footed North American mammal, *Oreamnos americanus*, that is not a true goat and, actually, according to *E. Americana*, a small antelope.

SMART GUY →

IGNORAMUS

daddy longlegs spider

a long-legged arachnid that's visibly similar to a spider, but visually different, having only one pair of eyes to the typical true spider's four; in other words, it looks like a spider, but it doesn't look like a spider.

foul pole

either of two vertical poles located at the outfield corners of a baseball playing field to separate fair territory from foul territory and the rowdies sitting in the bleachers (also called the cheap seats) from the more civilized fans; a ball that hits the foul pole is not a foul ball— and, for some reason, that just doesn't seem quite fair.

moth hole

a hole in a sweater that a moth might be able to fly through but not create, which is something only a moth-in-the-making larva can do.

centipede
a repulsive little segmented invertebrate of the phylum Arthropoda that can really make your skin crawl (especially when you find one crawling on your skin); the number of body segments varies among species, but every centipede has one pair of legs per segment, and the typical centipede creeps about on about 30 to 70 fewer legs than its name implies. (There are some foot-long, mouse-eating centipedes in the tropics with over 300 legs—but you don't really want to know about those.)

millipede
a creepy crawly cousin of the centipede that has two pairs of legs for every one of its segments; the typical millipede, however, still gets around on around 800 fewer legs than *its* name implies.

EVOLUTION

electric eel

a freshwater fish, *Electrophorus electricus*, that possesses special organs capable of producing a human-stunning 650 volts of electricity; related to the carps and minnows, it is not one of the true eels belonging to the fish order Apodes, at least not by current classifications.

jack rabbit   *Lepus californicus*, a long-eared hare (a member of a group of very antisocial mammals that are born covered with hair and that don't dig burrows) that's mislabeled a rabbit (a member of a group of very sociable hare relatives born totally naked and given to living in burrows they dig a lot with lots of other friendly bunnies), and that's one mistake that makes the jack rabbit hopping mad.

Belgian hare   a European rabbit that doesn't really care if it's called a hare.

horseshoe crab   any of several species of armor-plated marine arthropods that are closely related to spiders; if this "living fossil" hadn't remained virtually unchanged over the last 200 million years, it just might have evolved into a much more serious crab. Also mistitled **king crab.**

king crab   See **horseshoe crab.** Not to be confused with the *Alaska king crab,* which isn't a legitimate crab either.

hermit crab   any of numerous little marine animals that might have become crabs if they hadn't evolved into relatives of the lobster instead—and might not be spending all of their time squatting in vacant mollusk shells if they hadn't forgotten to evolve shells of their own along the way.

Greenland the world's largest island, 85% of which is covered by a permanent ice cap that's one mile thick and almost four times the size of France; only a tiny fraction of what isn't always under ice ever gets green, and that only happens for a couple of months each summer. (*Note:* Greenland was named in the 10th century by Eric the Red to encourage travelers stopping at Iceland to jump back in their boats and keep on going.)

Iceland

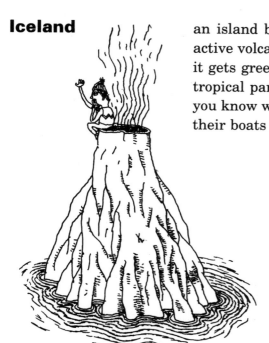

an island between Scandinavia and Greenland noted for its many active volcanoes and a few medium-sized glaciers; only about 25% of it gets green in the summertime, but compared to Greenland, it's a tropical paradise. (*Note:* Iceland was named in the 10th century by you know who to encourage travelers stopping there to jump back in their boats and head straight for Greenland.)

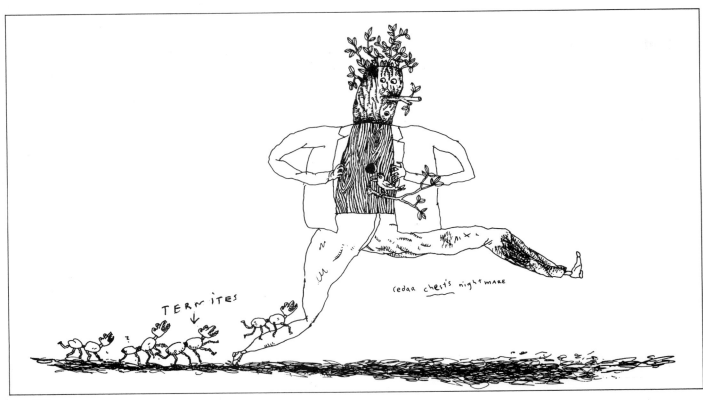

TERMITES

cedar chest's nightmare

52

cedar chest   a chest lined with the fragrant wood of the Eastern red cedar, *Juniperus virginiana*, a juniper tree of the cypress family, none of whose members are true cedars.

Cedar Rapids   a city in eastern, central Iowa that was originally called Rapids City for the turbulence of the stretch of river it is situated on and later renamed for all the *Juniperus virginiana* growing along that waterway, also misnamed for the tree.

game preserve an area of land set aside for the preservation of certain wild animals, so that they can be tracked down and killed by certain civilized individuals who think hunting is a big game; once quite numerous, these spurious sanctuaries are now bordering on extinction.

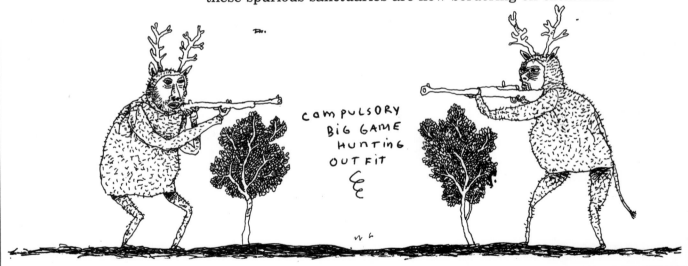

COMPULSORY
BIG GAME
HUNTING
OUTFIT

cyclone fence   a chain link fence that offers so little resistance to the wind it is able to remain standing even after being hit by the 400-mile-per-hour winds of a tornado, which is a pretty good indication that it will also hold up in the relatively lazy winds circulating around one of those large regions of low pressure called a cyclone.

cyclone cellar   a space where people hide from tornadoes, commonly found in the Midwest under houses surrounded by cyclone fences.

koala bear   a eucalyptus-munching, Australian marsupial whose name shouldn't have the word "bear" in it any more than Qantas, the airline the cuddly little koala so despises, should be spelled with a "u."

Douglas fir

a tree of western North America that's the fastest growing of all the evergreens (second only to the redwoods in reaching great heights), the most important source of lumber in the U.S., and not a real fir. (*Note:* Meticulous and exacting botanists have carefully and precisely classified the Douglas fir, calling it *Pseudotsuga*, which means "phony hemlock.")

Oregon pine

another *Pseudotsuga* pseudonym. Also erroneously called **Douglas spruce.**

Douglas spruce

See **Oregon pine.** Erroneously called **Douglas yew,** too.

World Series   a series of seven games played in October between the champions of the American League and the National League to determine the championship of the whole world, which, at the present time, includes only the United States and Canada.

light-year   a unit of length, not of a length of time; how far light travels in one year, about 6,000,000,000,000 miles, at a speed of 186,000 miles a second, which is fast enough to get you almost anywhere in a twinkle.

horned toad   *Phrynosoma cornutum*, the Texas horned toad, and any of several other outrageously ugly lizards.

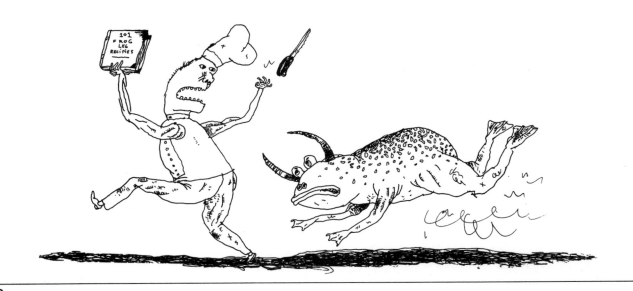

alligator shirt

Muffy and Skip's favorite, a short-sleeved, cotton-knit sportshirt that comes in all the right colors; misnamed for the French tennis star of the 30s, René Lacoste, it bears the famous little patch that recalls his reptilian nickname—and also makes the shirt rather a croc.

heart condition   the condition of your heart, whether it's a not-so-tip-top ticker about to take its last tock, or a real superpumper that seems like it's going to keep right on lubb-dupping a long way into the future.

Saturday Night Live   a late-night TV comedy review whose live skits are broadcast via tape after a seven-second delay, which is just long enough to miss some of the show's racier bits.

fairy tale   a tale that's nearly never told about or by fairies, and anyone who tells you different is telling you a real fairy tale.

circus seal

Also erroneously called **performing seal.** *Zalophus californicus*, a stage-struck sea lion whose external ears and large rear flippers that it can walk on clearly distinguish it from a real seal, even though it can do a socko seal impersonation given a big enough sardine.

gilt bronze

a very expensive material used to decorate furniture belonging to Marie Antoinette and Imelda Marcos, almost always made by fusing a layer of gold to a piece of cast brass. Also called **ormolu,** and, more recently, **Imeldamolu.**

enlarger

a device used in a photographic darkroom to project light through a negative in order to make a print that is larger than, the same size as, or even smaller than the negative. (*Note:* Prints made this way are normally a lot bigger than the negative, which does shed some light on how the enlarger's name developed.)

vitamin B₁₅

a substance of uncertain chemical composition, sometimes called "pangamic acid," sold as an organic nutrient that is required in the diet, usually in small amounts, for the normal functioning of the body and for the prevention of diseases caused by a deficiency in the nutrient, which is what a vitamin is, by definition, and what vitamin B₁₅ definitely is not.

vitamin B$_{17}$

an organic substance obtained from apricot pits that isn't needed in any amounts in the body. (*Note:* Formerly peddled under the name "Laetrile" as a cancer cure, this substance contains quite a bit of cyanide, and a vitamin B$_{17}$ deficiency may, in fact, result in a much longer, much healthier life.)

natural vitamin C

ascorbic acid ($C_6H_8O_6$), an organic substance needed in the diet for the normal functioning of the body and that is the same $C_6H_8O_6$ whether it's squeezed from an orange or a rose hip or whipped up in a laboratory (as distinguished from *supernatural vitamin C*, which, naturally, by definition doesn't exist).

64

Large olive   a small olive—compared to an Extra Large olive, that is.

Extra Large olive   a small olive—compared to a Mammoth olive, that is.

Mammoth olive   a small olive—compared to a Giant olive, that is.

Giant olive   a small olive—compared to a Jumbo olive, that is.

Jumbo olive   a small olive—compared to a Colossal olive, that is.

Colossal olive   a small olive—compared to a Super Colossal olive, that is.

Super Colossal olive   a large olive. Compare **Large olive**.

wild rice

grass seed from the once wild-growing but now widely cultivated *Zizania aquatica* (not to be confused with *Oryza sativa*, the long-tame plant that produces the more than 7,000 varieties of true rice, the grass seed thrown at weddings).

rice paper   paper made from the pithy part of the stems of *Tetrapanax papyri-ferum*, commonly called the rice-paper tree; the notion that it's made from rice is just silly, because there isn't a grain of truth to it.

RICE PAPER

strawberry not a berry; not even *a* fruit; the juicy swollen end of a strawberry stem in which a whole bunch of individual fruits (ripened ovaries) are embedded. (*Note:* Tomatoes, cucumbers, watermelons, grapes, bananas, oranges, and eggplants—all of them ripened plant ovaries with mature fleshy walls—are bona fide berries. A blueberry is also a true berry, a true-blue berry, and a blue true berry.)

drycell battery a kind of electrical battery normally not included with battery-operated toys and containing an electrolytic chemical paste that is occasionally dry; on such occasions, however, the battery is considered dead.

funny bone a nerve, the ulnar, not a bone, in the elbow, which, especially when hit, is not the least bit funny.

limited edition the entire number of copies of an item, such as a collector thimble, commemorative dolly, or painfully pretty print, produced in a prodigious quantity, limited only by the number of suckers sucked into sending away for the item, by a mass marketer whose business is based on selling as many of whatever he's churning out to as many people as possible. (*Note:* This term was formerly used exclusively for editions of fine prints produced in quantities that it didn't take a minicomputer to count. The way it's used today really is the limit.)

fabric softener a substance added to a washer or dryer in order to add a greasy, lubricating coating to the fibers of fabrics so that they feel softer without actually being softer; a slick product description if ever there was one.

Montreal Expos   a National League baseball team that plays out of Montreal, Canada, and doesn't have a single player from Montreal or even Canada; most Expo fans, however, *are* from Montreal, and now they know how American hockey fans used to feel.

Toronto Blue Jays   See **Montreal Expos** (and read "American" for "National," "Toronto" for "Montreal," and "Blue Jay" for "Expo").

french fries   deep-fried potato strips, originally introduced into France by the Belgians, and recently reintroduced into France by McDonald's.

Big Mac® a real McNomer, and here's the beef: meatwise, it's maybe one of the world's smallest hamburgers, and not calling it a Big Mc makes it an even bigger whopper.

horsepower

a standard unit used for measuring the power of an engine or motor; one horsepower is equal to the power required to lift 550 pounds one foot in one second, a task that today would take at least one and a half healthy horses to accomplish—which just goes to prove that the old gray mare she ain't what she used to be.

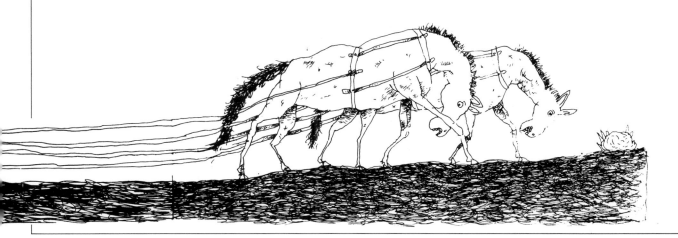

killer whale   *Orcinus orca*, a large dolphin (which makes it a smallish type of whale) that feeds on fish, birds, and sometimes even other marine mammals, some of whom also feed on fish, birds, and sometimes other marine mammals but don't get called killers on account of their diets. (*Note:* Hunted in the wild for its meat and oil by killer humans from Norway and Japan, the large-brained killer whale is very docile and even playful in captivity—positive proof that while it can be a little aggressive at times, it certainly isn't stupid.)

hardwood   wood from broad-leaved deciduous trees, regardless of how hard or soft it happens to be; balsa wood, which is so soft you can practically cut it with a butter knife, is a hardwood.

softwood   wood from cone-bearing, needle-leaved evergreen trees, regardless of how soft or hard it happens to be; Georgia pine, so hard you can use it to hammer nails (even into some so-called hardwoods a whole lot harder than balsa), is a softwood.

shooting star another name for a meteor that's popular but not especially bright.

shooting
STAR

saber-toothed tiger

a large feline with very large canines that would probably be even longer in the tooth today if it hadn't run out of lives around 10,000 years ago; it is no more closely related to modern-day tigers than it is to lions, leopards, or the world's millions of tabby-toothed Morrises.

simple majority   a number of votes acquired by a candidate in an election that is greater than the number of votes won by any one of two or more other candidates running in the same contest but not necessarily greater than the number of votes obtained by all of those candidates combined, which sure doesn't sound any simpler than just beating the pants off only one other candidate.

NATIONAL COALITION OF SIMPLE MINDED PEOPLE WHO ALL SHARE THE SAME DUMB OPINION

crystal

(as in *crystal saltshaker*) a superior type of glass (a solid material whose atoms are randomly arranged) often cut to create facets resembling the geometric planes of real crystals (solids composed of atoms arranged in regularly repeating patterns), like the crystals of salt in a crystal saltshaker.

Barbary ape

a monkey whose reputation as an ape is as solid as the rock of Gibraltar—which also happens to be one of the places where it lives.

book club

a booklovers' group that holds no regular meetings and doesn't even have a clubhouse; members are usually drubbed out if they don't comply with the club's buylaws.

10-gallon hat   a cowboy hat with a very high crown that, at most, might hold close to a gallon—still a lot of water on the brain.

World War I

a conflict that took place between 1914 and 1918, involving many but not all of the nations of the world. Also erroneously called **the war to end all wars.**

World War II

a conflict that took place between 1939 and 1945, involving many but not all of the nations of the world.

World War III

the first real world war, a conflict that might take an hour or two, total, sometime in the future, involving all of the nations of the world whether they want to be involved or not. More appropriately called **the war to end all wars . . . and everything else as well.**

the dictionary   (as in, "According to *the* dictionary. . .") a legendary lexicon containing everything you ever wanted to know about every word in the English language, as distinguished from less-reverential references, including *The Oxford English Dictionary, Webster's Third New International Dictionary, The Random House Dictionary of the English Language, The American Heritage Dictionary*, and *Webster's New World Dictionary*, that must have to look up all their words in *the* dictionary, too.

index

Official Misnomers Entry Blank

Dear Mark & Diane:

Here's my mistaken identifier and the reason why I think it should be yanked from *the* dictionary (and from all those *other* dictionaries, too) right away:

_____

_____

_____

_____

_____

All the best,

name _____

street address _____

city, state, zip code _____

Misnomers
P.O. Box 7713
New York, NY 10150